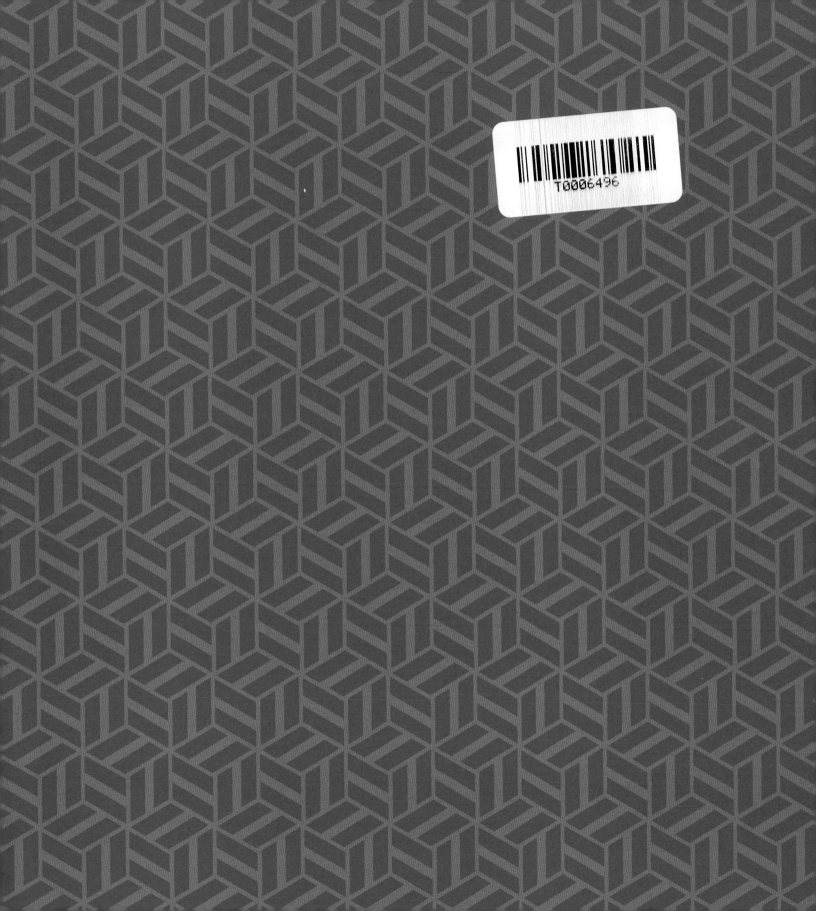

dream rooms for
children

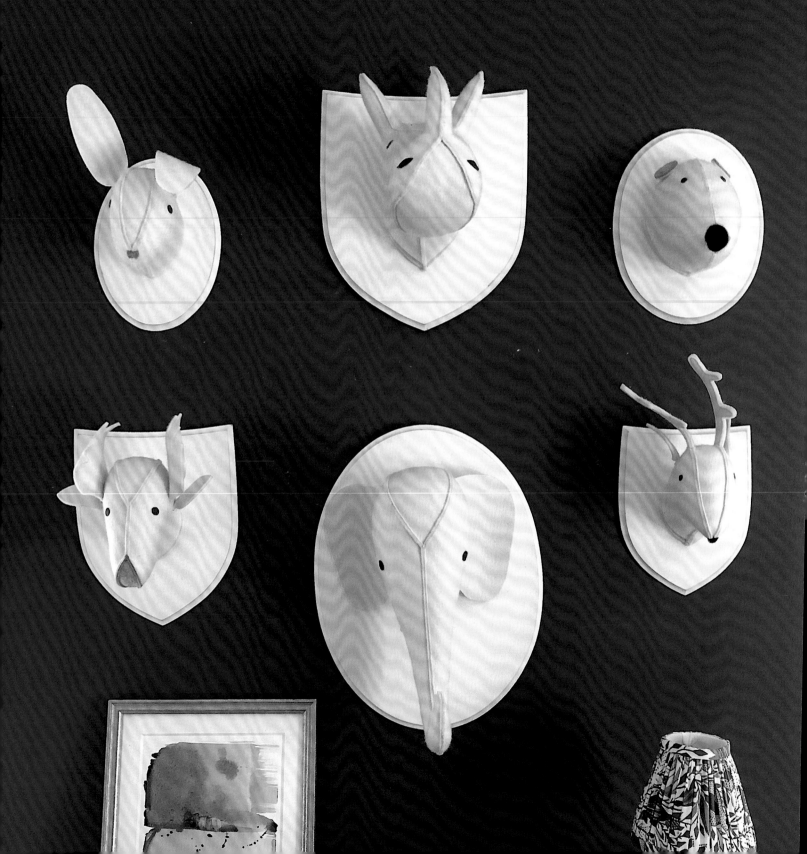

dream rooms for children

imaginative spaces to sleep, study, and play

susanna salk

RIZZOLI
NEW YORK

New York Paris London Milan

contents

introduction *by* susanna salk

My two sons now hover over me and I am almost six feet tall. So while the memories of buying a crib or bunk beds or posters of music idols for their rooms are as amorphous as the ones stemming from my own childhood domain, the excitement of adapting their present rooms—that patiently wait for them like empty park benches as they live away— still delights as it did when they were small enough for me to scoop into my arms and read them to sleep.

For children's rooms are not just about the present days, they are about the tomorrows. How can their rooms of today nurture them into the grown people they will become?

When we moved into our current house a few years ago, my teenage son Winston, who was then living nearby at boarding school, was determined to transform his small bedroom into a place where he could retreat in style on the weekends. From his dorm room he texted me a photo from the '70s of a living space that can be best described as a place where James Bond might relax between assignments.

A few days later his sketch followed, of how he imagined a platform bed could be built out from the wall, flush between long window seats on either side. A design dialogue started to flow that eventually included our carpenter and the space was soon realized, complete with blue velvet seat cushions, a TV screen stemming out from the wall, framed vintage movie posters, and a landscape painting snagged at Goodwill for twenty-five bucks. It's not just his cocoon, it's become his style passport.

My original book *Room for Children: Stylish Spaces for Sleep and Play*, was born from the realization that we as a culture were starting to embrace the philosophy—not to mention the aesthetics—that children's areas deserved to be places that didn't stagnate in the stage where the children were at that very moment. Basic primary colors and fairy tale and super hero characters were ceding to sophisticated patterns and unique color hues and vintage furniture with dashes of whimsy. Children were being given more of a center stage

in their little worlds at home and those worlds in turn were aesthetically on par with the adult spaces in the rest of the house.

Almost ten years later, as I compile some of my favorite spaces for children again, (for there's a whole fresh crop of babies, toddlers, and teens!) I see we have moved the boundaries even farther without losing our sense of fun and practicality. I see rooms that identify a child as a whole child, not necessarily only by gender. I see workspaces that cohabitate cleverly within play spaces, thanks to open minds and open planning. I see that children have had an even greater hand in their room's creation and I see parents telling designers how important it is to them that their newborn's space adapt to their baby's eventual growth, both physically and emotionally. I see dining room furniture placed below framed children's drawings and I see rocking chairs placed alongside blue chip modern art. There aren't just two brands or colors for cribs, there are hundreds. I see bunk beds worthy of luxury cruise ships. But the most repeated word by both designers and parents when describing their intent at fashioning these spaces is "timeless." Parents want spaces that can adapt and accommodate whatever the future may bring. Because when it comes to our children, we may give them time-outs but in the end, there is never enough time with them before they leave.

The phrase "empty nest" implies that when one's grown children leave the home, the home is then empty. But I believe that a home is as alive as we the parents who still live in it.

For you never stop being a parent. You want your children's rooms to be able to welcome them when they come home and remind them that you are there to give them their space, but also to give them shelter.

While researching images for this book, I came across a bedroom in a Brooklyn apartment for two young siblings: at the far end of the wall was a smoky mural of trees and clouds. It gave a dramatic destination to the small space. Cassandra Warner, its designer, as well as parent to two children (not to mention photographer of the space) kindly gave me the online resource for the

A downstairs guest room in the Brooklyn home of Cassandra Warner and Jeremy Floto is also a dreamy destination for their two young girls' playtime. "It's a quiet, open space that allows for the exuberance of life with small children to unfold in all its messy glory," says Floto. "The color palette is muted and gray with uncluttered furnishings. The wallpaper is Etched Arcadia wallpaper mural by Anthropologie Home. The walls are skimmed in cement mixed with pigment for warm undertones.

FLOTO+WARNER

digital wallpaper—another wonderful newer invention for parents and finicky kids!—and it suddenly made me want it for Winston's room.

When I called Winston to ask what he thought, he was rushing between college classes on the West Coast but told me to send a picture. I sent a follow-up text of both the Brooklyn room and a swatch from the wallpaper's web site. In seconds, he replied: "Go for it!"

Within days, my husband and I were rolling out the sticky printed sheets to create the virtual forest within the real Connecticut one just outside those walls. Stepping back to view it from the threshold, the pastoral effect was as compelling as in the picture: it made you want to enter and then linger. And isn't that what we long for our children to do when they come home after their adventures?

starting off
nurs

eries

stylishly

design tips

"The reality is, the nursery should be designed for the mother not the baby and that should be the focus. We always try to select a plush rocking chair to keep the mother and baby comfortable during feedings. Happy mom, happy baby." —louisa g. roeder

"You want a narrative for a child's bedroom that inspires growth spiritually, spatially, and creatively. Simplicity is key." —stefania skrabak

"A daybed is a must-have as it is the perfect piece for both early morning snuggles and late night feedings. It's a nice place for an adult to watch the child as well as for the child to transition to the crib." —griffith roth

"Most people decorate a nursery with solely the child in mind. One must not forget that the nursery must also be a happy place for the parent—a place to find some respite especially in the early years. It should be a feel-good place for all who enter—especially tired parents and caregivers!" —tilton fenwick

"A nursery is almost meant to be a fantasy room—the parents' dream realized. As the children get older, we encourage their involvement in personalizing their rooms. Designing a nursery is often about color, an important consideration in creating a calm, cozy, happy place for a child to live and play in." —alex papachristidis

"Kids' rooms are an area where no one is usually willing to break the bank. We love finding one element and doing it well. Find something with scale and color and make it the focal point. Make it playful and fun and no one will notice you didn't splurge on the full-length triple-lined curtains and custom rug." —ashley whittaker

South Carolina-based designer Angie Hranowsky floated the crib in front of the windows to allow for plenty of rocking time and playing on the rug. The parent, who is an artist, worked with Hranowsky to create a custom wallpaper based on one of their paintings. "I selected the green paint to pull from the colors in the print, but also to add some depth," says Hranowsky. "I wanted to stay away from the expected color palette of a common nursery." The zebra rug graphic breaks up the traditional architecture of the nineteenth-century house and creates juxtaposition with the floral patterns on the walls and cornice.

ANGIE HRANOWSKY

"This nursery holds an extra special place in my heart as it belongs to my daughter Emma," says designer Melissa Warner Rothblum. "I wanted to create something that could grow with her—serene but with pops of color and a little spunk." To help the nursery always look tidy, Rothblum opted for enclosed storage made to look like a large dollhouse instead of an open bookshelf, so there's room for everything but it can be stored neatly away. The chic bins under the crib are easy to access for the baby but also keep toys organized.

MELISSA WARNER ROTHBLUM

"It's rare for the window treatments in a room to be the showstopper, however, these Pierre Frey shades are the exception that dominate this room," says New York-based designer Louisa Roeder. "We did not want to distract from them, so we avoided all bold patterns and bright colors. And we repeated the fabric again in the crib's bumper, further emphasizing the focus on the shades."

LOUISA G. ROEDER

"I like to call this space, A Nursery Fit for
the Prince of Camo-lot," says Cara Boyce of
Red Wagon Design. "It was created for my client's
third (and final, she thinks) child and first boy.
We wanted to celebrate traditional ideas of boyhood
in a unique and fun way that would grow with him
through toddlerhood and beyond." Using Philip
Gorrivan's Desert Storm wallpaper pattern on the
ceiling gave Boyce an opportunity to do something
bold and fun without overwhelming the space.
"It offers an unexpected detail and something engaging
for our little client to look up at from his crib."

CARA BOYCE, RED WAGON DESIGN

This family wanted a nursery wallpaper that would last through their baby's teenage years. Boston-based Kristine Mullaney smartly chose Alan Campbell's pattern Zig Zag, which, thanks to its playfully cool vibe, will stand the test of time. She then matched the paint's trim to the brighter navy color in the wallpaper, a small detail that makes a big impact even in a child's little years.

KRISTINE MULLANEY DESIGN

Who says a crib must be white? The modern gray of
this one anchors the nursery and the pale walls act
as a gallery-like backdrop for a whimsical display of
personal touches and treasures. "We created this room
originally for our son when he was a newborn, with the
intention of it growing with him," says Joe Williamson
of the Hollymount design firm. "He is now six-years-old
and it is basically the same! We wanted lots of texture
and convertible pieces that made the room feel layered
and interesting—not like a typical 'kid' room." Deer soft
sculpture by Hollymount, carpet from ABC Carpet &
Home, and crib/changing table from Oeuf.

HOLLYMOUNT

"I wanted my son's room to feel like a moment from a storybook," says New York-based designer Stefania Skrabak. "I envisioned a sleepy cabin in the woods and a secret reading nook within, as if at any moment, friendly forest creatures could scamper off the pages and join us for bedtime stories." To achieve this, Skrabak went with simplicity in natural textures and patterns—from the wallpaper quality of the birch veneer on the sliding doors, to the knots from the pine on the ceiling, to the woven patterns of the carpets and bedding. The sconces are from Restoration Hardware and the walls are painted in Lowe's White Barn.

STEFANIA SKRABAK OF AHG INTERIORS, ART HOME GARDEN, LLC

"Since my client is playful by nature, they wanted the room to be fun and a bit unconventional," says Los Angeles-based designer Ross Cassidy. "I wanted to put my unique spin on the ubiquitous stuffed giraffe by giving it a purpose instead of it being merely decorative, so I hung a 1960s French mobile from his mouth." As the baby grows up, the navy, white, and beige color scheme Cassidy implemented (with its painted grass cloth wall coverings) won't need to change as it works as well for a newborn as it will for a teenager.

ROSS CASSIDY

A sophisticated circus tent-like atmosphere gives a baby delight when looking upwards in this nursery with a gender-neutral palette. "This room is in a two bedroom apartment that also needed to function as the home office," says its California-based designer Kari McIntosh. "The West Elm secretary stores their laptop equipment and paper filing system." The Oeuf crib was selected for its use of non-toxic materials and ability to convert as the child grows. Chair and ottoman repurposed from the family and re-covered in LuluDK for Schumacher.

KARI MCINTOSH DESIGN

"I always want to create a child's space that feels whimsical and young, but can also grow with them over time, hopefully into their teens," says designer Palmer Weiss. "Wall decals for art can be useful, especially as they can be replaced with something more age appropriate as the baby grows up. More importantly, they can be a solution in earthquake territory, where decorating over a crib in a responsible way can be a struggle. Carpet is by Moquette and crib is Netto Collection.

PALMER WEISS

Mais les crocodilles aiment s'amuser un peu

J·P·R

PORTER

GOODNIGHT MOON

Meet The Little Prince

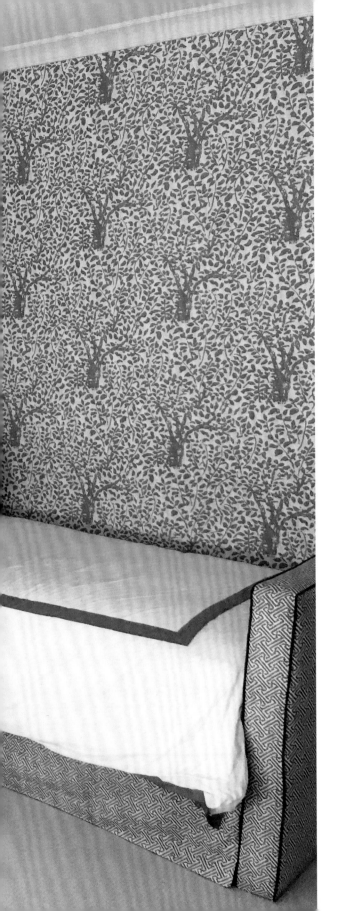

"We wanted this nursery to feel fresh with whimsical touches that appealed to a child's curiosity," says designer Griffith Roth of Griffith Blythe Interiors. "Babies and young children love pattern so we chose the iconic Billy Baldwin Arbre de Matisse wallpaper in French Blue by Quadrille. Through art and objects, the playful elements were added. The giraffe is both sculptural and a guardian of the child's crib. A happy room makes for a happy child!"

GRIFFITH BLYTHE INTERIORS

"With its unexpected details and layers of pattern, we wanted this space to be unique and playful," says Jennie Bishop of Studio Gild. "The neutral palette and sophisticated furnishings allow for the room to grow with the child, from toddler to teen. All you'd need to do is switch the crib to a bed!" For the two-year-old currently living in the space, the shelves were fastened to the wall so a possible climb attempt wouldn't be a double disaster. A furry rug is gentle on little knees and a few oversize beanbags are pillows for lounging and reading. The wallpaper is from Cole & Sons and the crib is Spot on Square.

JENNIE BISHOP FOR STUDIO GILD

Designer Lisa Sherry's client had a very clear aesthetic vision for their child's nursery: "They wanted a calm, neutral environment, feminine but not too girlie. So I looked to nature," says Sherry. "The woodsy branch-and-leaf papier-mâché chandelier puts a new spin on a traditional mobile as does the rabbit decal peeking over the side of the crib." Underfoot, Sherry specified a pink graphic rug, soft enough for a future crawler, and topped it with a quirky faux bearskin.

LISA SHERRY OF LISA SHERRY INTERIEURS

Given its tiny size, designer Hannah Soboroff Shargal of EEMA Studio was challenged creating a soothing space for a newborn. Undaunted, she turned a closet into a sleeping nook by removing its doors and then lining the walls with Coven wallpaper by Maison C. The oval mini Stokke crib starts out as a bassinet and can grow into a full-size crib.

HANNAH SOBOROFF SHARGAL, EEMA STUDIO

"This room was designed with both the newborn and new parents in mind," says San Francisco-based designer Dina Bandman, who drew inspiration from her travels to Italy's Amalfi coast with its prolific lemon trees. "I wanted to create a gender-neutral nursery and when a green and yellow color palette came to mind, I collaborated with de Gournay to create a new sequin-embellished Lemon Grove wallpaper entirely for this room." Bandman also fashioned the exquisite four poster Lucite crib to enhance, rather than compete, with the room's fresh and fanciful design. "My design intention is for baby to nestle in style and for parents to feel uplifted and energized in this special nursery."

DINA BANDMAN INTERIORS

spaces designed

bedr

ooms

for dreams

design tips

"My favorite trick for a child this age is a custom twin and half mattress. It is in between the size of a full and twin and allows a little extra room for a sleepover friend without taking up too much space in a room. Full sheets fit fine so no custom linens are needed." —palmer weiss

"Children grow up very quickly, so their rooms should offer solutions that are ageless and age appropriate for all years. Flexible, hidden storage in a child's room is particularly important, so the space can look tidy quickly." —amy lau

"You always apply the same skills to a child's room as you would to any other room in the house: you want it to function and be comfortable and endure." —miles redd

"I always request to meet with the children whose rooms I'm designing. They are who create the inspiration for their own rooms. The look on their faces when they first walk into the rooms says it all." —julie hillman

"Kids don't care so much about furniture arrangements: just chairs floating and some empty space to play is what counts. And a white rug is like a blank canvas for Legos." —david netto

"When designing a bunk room, it's essential to balance practicality, safety, comfort, and whimsy. We make sure that ladders are scaled and pitched ergonomically for both children and adults." —bradley stephens

"Design kids' rooms so that they grow with the child. Spend more on furniture and case goods that are functional and fun and let bedding and age-specific details that will wear with time come from more value-priced sources." —ma allen

"I always have our clients with children make sure to have the furniture and carpets sealed by a company like Solutions, who we use in Los Angeles, to protect from the inevitable stains." —joe lucas

previous pages and opposite: In her Dominican Republic retreat, designer Celerie Kemble conjures up a family playroom (complete with extra bedding) that feels equal parts fantasy and familiar. The papier-mâché masks on the walls are by local teenagers, many of whom were winners in the annual Carnival mask contest held in Río San Juan. "They set the tone," says Kemble. "I wanted fanciful without feeling babyish." The wicker bed, chairs, coffee table, and turtle table were found though various flea markets and vintage vendors and then shipped to the island. Kemble designed the ceiling light. "Wacky never dates itself," she says.

CELERIE KEMBLE, KEMBLE INTERIORS, INC

This is a child's bedroom in the country, where she spends weekends and holidays. "We wanted it to reflect the country setting and used our Gibbie pattern from Robert Allen Duralee in Aqua all over the walls to envelope the space," says designer Anne Maxwell Foster of Tilton Fenwick, the firm she runs with her partner Suysel dePedro Cunningham. "We also added a printed wallpaper to the ceiling and painted the trim; it was all about being out of the harsh city and into a soft and cozy country bedroom." The design duo opted for huge slide out drawers under the Ducduc bed for toy storage and easy cleaning up at night.

SUYSEL DEPEDRO CUNNINGHAM & ANNE MAXWELL FOSTER OF TILTON FENWICK

For this young family's beach house, architect Matt Benson and designer Barrie Benson created a bunk room full of storage, beds, and fun with an obvious nod to vintage sailboats. The overscaled portholes house beds, secret storage, and reading lights for six children as well as a hidden closet with storage drawers for duffels. Concealed drawers below portholes pull out with additional beds for cousins, friends, and dogs.

BARRIE BENSON INTERIOR DESIGN

Providing separate work and sleep spaces for two children, ages six and ten, was as important as maximizing a play space that could last beyond their early childhood years. Case in point: the sofa now occupies the space that held the former changing table. "We prioritize adaptability—especially in family homes," says its architect, Tim Barber, who created the space with designer Kristen Panitch.

TIM BARBER, PRINCIPAL ARCHITECT, TIM BARBER, LTD, AND KRISTEN PANITCH INTERIORS

In this beach house, designer Sara Gilbane wanted her own five-year-old son's bedroom to reflect his personality: bold and fun. "I also wanted it to grow with him and to have some special pieces that would be his forever," she says. "The quilt is vintage, and mixed with the D Porthault stars-patterned bedding it hides everything! It all just sings together. The modern art on the wall are basic shapes in strong blue colors that suit the mood perfectly."

SARA GILBANE

This cozy Brooklyn-based bedroom room for two young boys becomes more dynamic (and feels larger) thanks to its removable Chasing Paper's Green Leaf print on its once white walls. "We wanted to create a fun, bright room that felt like an escape to somewhere warm and that also included books and art that would inspire our boys," says David A. Land.

DAVID A. LAND AND RUMAAN ALAM

For a lucky infant, designer Tamara
Magel used a Gucci wallpaper that
instantly sets the right mood. "Its vivid
pattern is serious yet playful," says
Magel. The white furniture complements
perfectly and offers serene pops of
glamour. Daybed from Oly.

TAMARA MAGEL DESIGN

A tiger seems to keep watch over this room's tender occupant and gives gentle drama to a bedroom. A fearlessly bold rug—this one by Edward Barber and Jay Osgerby for The Rug Company—is a great way to bring style to a young space and it can easily adapt to future tastes either by moving it to another room or by pairing it with a more grown-up wallpaper.

"I wanted to create a charming and cheerful room that evoked a tech-free childhood, a place for my son to play in that was cozy and livable and not precious," says New York-based designer Starrett Ringbom. "When he moved into the room he was only three-years-old, so he was—and remains—enchanted by the characters and horses in the Brunschwig et Fils Battle of Valmy wallpaper." Ringbom covered his bed in Sunbrella fabric not only due to its cheerful nature but also because she says, "it's indestructible!"

STARRETT RINGBOM

77

"I loved the idea of an artist-made rug since the owners are art collectors," says interior designer Julie Hillman. "Their daughter chose this Damien Hirst rug." Hillman framed the expansive view with custom curtains by Manhattan Shade and Associates that came with big personality. The bold graphic lines of the curtains are a nice contrast to the spiral rug.

JULIE HILLMAN DESIGN

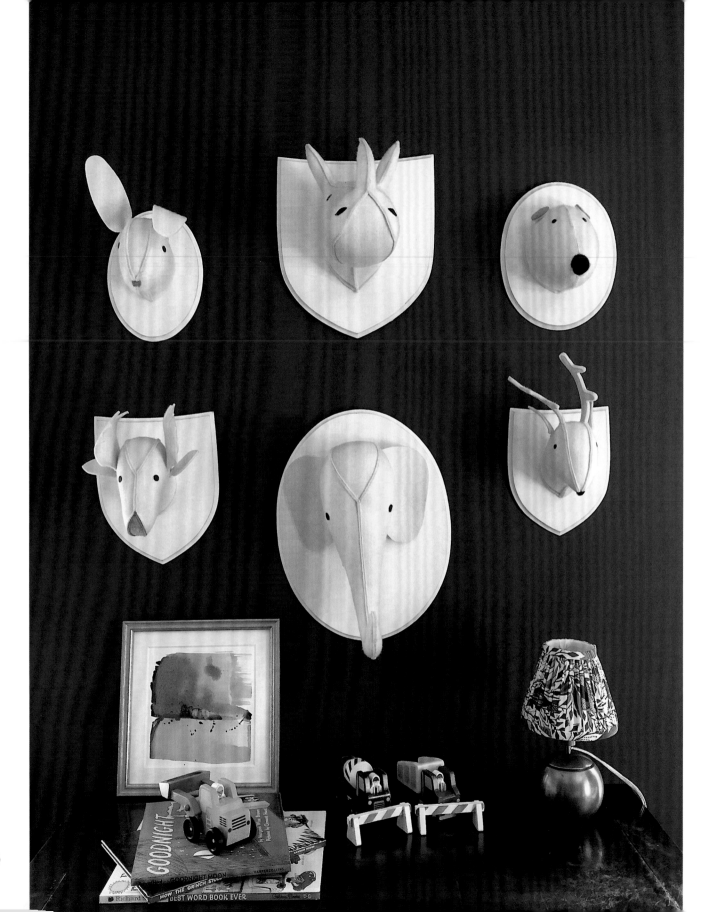

Farrow & Ball's Stiffkey Blue is just the right
backdrop for a three-year-old boy's room.
"I used a deep blue color for the walls, which
creates a cozy environment for my son to
relax and play in, while complementing the
bold Mongolian rug that covers most of the
space," say his mother, designer Debbie Propst.
The wool felt animal heads are from RH Baby
& Child: "Not only are they a playful nod to the
modern farmhouse aesthetic of the rest of my
home," says Propst, "but I love the charm and
sense of humor they convey—something that's
always important to me while decorating."

**DEBBIE PROPST, ONE KINGS LANE
INTERIOR DESIGN**

"When it came to creating a bedroom for my two daughters, I thought about what I wanted as a child but didn't have," says London designer Beata Heuman. "It was mainly a princess bed, so that had to be part of the scheme. I worked with a specialist painter to create a hand-painted mural inspired by Bemelmans Bar at the Carlyle Hotel in New York. I love the naughty hares smoking cigars and drinking martinis. Yes, they are cute, but they also have some edge, and the children enjoy gazing at the characters and weaving their own stories about what mischief they are up to! It has ended up being one of my favorite rooms in our house."

BEATA HEUMAN

In this bedroom for a girl in Portugal, Maria Barros was asked by the ten-year-old to create a wallpaper mural of wish ribbons from Brazil, each *fitinhas* having a happy memory on it from the girl's life. Barros also wove in some of her client's favorite strong colors (blue being one of them) in clean pops throughout the space, from the sofa piping to the hexagon wallpaper behind the homework area. The result is an unexpectedly modern space that feels deeply personal.

MARIA BARROS HOME

"Vintage or new textiles from India, Mexico, or Ukraine make for wonderful headboards," says designer Fawn Galli. Here for a seven-year-old boy, she choose a vintage textile from John Robshaw. "Textiles with age are more soulful and unique. When I travel I am always on the hunt for new and vintage textiles."

FAWN GALLI INTERIORS

For an extended family of five young cousins between eight and fourteen years, this bunk room is a favorite place for sleepovers, even for adult guests when the house is full for holidays and busy summer weekends. The room sleeps eight on the twin bunks, and three on twin-size trundles. "The clients asked me to design a bunk room that is not only comfortable and inviting, but one that could sleep more than any of their friends' bunk rooms," says designer Bradley Stephens of Stephens Design Group. "Their goal is to have the house where all the kids want to hang out. The spacious room with vaulted ceilings allowed us to build three walls of substantial bunks that feel like nooks with amenities like upholstered side and back panels, individual reading sconces, and built-in backgammon and chess tables. We wanted the structures to be grand and inspiring, with nautical lines and railings like an ocean liner. The materials are rich and reflect the sophistication of the rest of the house." Leather-wrapped hardware by Turnstyle Designs. The walls are papered in a beachy stripe by Farrow & Ball.

BRADLEY STEPHENS, PRINCIPAL, STEPHENS DESIGN GROUP

"I designed this room for my son Jasper when he was twelve," says Cathy Bailey. It's a place where sleep or music can all happen, thanks to Bailey's thoughtful placement and no nonsense organization that doesn't take itself too seriously. A long wall is an opportunity to create extra storage and ideal surface space for homework.

**CATHY BAILEY FOR
HEATH CERAMICS**

91

"It's pretty impossible to wake up in this room and have a bad day," says designer Jessica Geller of her five-year-old daughter Lola's bedroom. "I love the architecture of this attic space and I wanted to highlight the roofline and the crescent windows. If we left the ceiling painted, it would only draw your eye to the solid flat ceiling because the angles of the walls lead your eye straight up. Swathing the room in Pierre Frey's Arty on all surfaces creates a cozy cocoon. And this particular pattern works well because it is nondirectional."

TOLEDO GELLER INTERIORS

Art, color, and distinct furniture all
can play equal parts in creating
a space for a child that feels unique
and spurs their imagination.

POPHAM DESIGN

"As our firm often does, we splurged
on items that would stay with this
ten-year-old girl over the years, such
as the Katie Ridder wallpaper," says
designer Bella Mancini, "but we saved in
places where she might outgrow them,
such as the bed from Crate&Kids."

BELLA MANCINI DESIGN

It's never too early to teach a child how to display their treasures with thought and style. The better it looks, the more effort they will make to clean up.

DIANA RICE AND CHELSEA REALE OF SISSY+MARLEY

Virginia-based designer Nancy Twomey
creates a stunning family space that
multitasks. Thanks to the streamlined
architecture and furniture, children get
to enjoy cozy bunk beds and during
playtime both children and parents
benefit from the stunning river views.

**NANCY TWOMEY OF FINNIAN
INTERIORS + FINNIAN'S MOON**

"The goal was to find the sweet spot between a space that wasn't too precious or too mature," says Rosemary Wormley of Ash Street Interiors, based in Illinois. "We wanted two beds so there would be room for sleepovers, but the room had an offset window that made symmetry difficult." The firm used the drapery cornices above the beds to conceal one of the windows and give the room glamorous punch. The wall color was custom, devised in part by the nine-year-old girl who sleeps there.

ASH STREET INTERIORS

For young sisters, a layered bedroom was created by designer Elizabeth Hay that feels both ethnic and modern, thanks to a variety of colorful and cozy patterns. "We used a variety in different scales to create a layered look that doesn't conflict," says Hay. Quadrille wallpaper, Lisa Fine headboard fabric, and Molly Mahon fabric on cushions. Handmade lampshades by Elizabeth Hay Design.

ELIZABETH HAY DESIGN

A daybed serves as invaluable seating in a nursery, with the intention that a young child can grow into it and use it as a bed with a soft back to lean against once the crib has been outgrown. The ladder with blankets is a functional way to add more dimension and texture to the room.

DEBBIE PROPST, ONE KINGS LANE INTERIOR DESIGN

"There's a very dignified colonial fireplace in this room and so I had this Founding Fathers wallpaper custom-made by Quadrille to 'complete' that idea, but in a fun way," says Los Angeles-based designer David Netto, who worked on this Hamptons, New York bedroom for a five-year-old boy. "The Kjaerholm PK-31 leather chairs give a sense of discipline and structure. They're already kind of beat up so nobody has to worry, and it's sort of surprising to find something so good in here. Surprises are important in design." The painting is a portrait of the child's grandfather.

INTERIOR DESIGN BY DAVID NETTO
ARCHITECTURE BY
HOTTENROTH & JOSEPH

A vacation home in Vero Beach, Florida was an opportunity to create a vibrant and fun space for a teenage girl. "Although she loves color, she wanted quiet walls so we selected a Philip Jeffries grass cloth in a natural color to add texture in lieu of paint," says Ashley Warren of the McCann Design Group. "We added a soft pink paint to the ceiling, which softens the room and coordinates with the fabrics." Quadrille and Peter Dunham fabrics and Oomph side table.

SARA MCCANN AND ASHLEY WARREN FOR MCCANN DESIGN GROUP

A four-year-old girl craved both pink and red for her new room, and designer Cameron Ruppert wanted to give her something she would be happy in for years to come but that was also punchy and fun with pops of color. "Once the window treatment fabric from Clarence House in their pattern Batyr was determined, I realized the dresser and the mirror from her old nursery went with the colorful but eclectic vibe I was going for," says Ruppert.

CAMERON RUPPERT INTERIORS

In Nantucket, a bunk room in a basement is ideal for a family's growing children and their friends. To make the room feel less like a basement, the owners made sure the ceilings were high and used window wells to get as much natural light as possible. The floors were also washed with a light stain and the walls were painted white to further lighten up the space. The small lamps by each bunk ensure that anyone who wants to curl up and read a book can do so. Multiple peg hooks for clothes and wet towels and the drawers under the bunk beds are used for extra blankets, luggage, and storage.

"This room in Crested Butte, Colorado, was created to accommodate kids of all ages so we used queen, full, and twin beds to maximize sleeping areas in the space of a historic building," says Florida-based designer Jett Thompson, who made sure to install charging stations and reading lights into each nook. "For those brave enough to scale the ladder, the top is like a secret fort with a Lego Playroom and beanbag chairs."

JETT THOMPSON HOME

"I wanted a room that reflected my daughter's lively spirit," says Katie Brown, "and embraced her love of pink and purple and all animals. I also wanted it to embrace the traditional architecture of the room but have it lean into the modern in order to update it a smidge." Brown purposefully found a low chest of drawers so her daughter could reach, put away, and pick out her own clothes. The wallpaper is by Antonia Vella for York.

KATIE BROWN AND THE KATIE BROWN WORKSHOP WITH THE HELP OF BRICE GILLARD AND STEPHANIE DITULLIO

"We wanted this room to have a clear direction for this eight-year-old girl's color preferences," says New York-based designer Bella Mancini. "But we also wanted it to feel collected. The exotic headboard is actually from Serena and Lily but I loved that it looks like something that came from family or travels. It gives so much texture to the room and adds something a plain headboard cannot."

BELLA MANCINI DESIGN

121

This is the room of a seven-year-old girl who loves to host sleepovers. "I wanted her BFF to have a matching twin for when she came over," says designer Lisa Sherry, "and the rest of the room is sleeping bag ready!" Wallcovering and duvet from John Robshaw.

LISA SHERRY OF LISA SHERRY INTERIEURS

For a ten-year-old boy, North Carolina-based designer Barrie Benson used the father's heirloom twin beds as a kick off point. "We wanted to lighten up the traditional and pack a punch with graphic stripes and pattern." Benson firmly believes in the power of a good nightstand—these are from Bungalow 5—with lots of storage. "It allows for toys and trinkets to remain out of sight." Her no-fuss bedding also stylishly sets up success when it's time to make the bed. "Many times I mix stripes and patterns as well as play around with balancing the strength of color," says Benson. "As long as I have a color thread or a change in scale of stripes to geometrics, the balance works."

BARRIE BENSON INTERIOR DESIGN

"Our little client, who was five at the time, is fascinated with buildings and the color red," says Chelsea Reale of New York-based design team Sissy+Marley. "So we made sure these key elements were a part of the design plan, including a house closet from This is Dutch that is ideal for storage." Babyletto Lemonade table and chairs.

DIANA RICE AND CHELSEA REALE OF SISSY+MARLEY

"We wanted to create a happy room with a bit of fantasy and playfulness," says New York-based designer Miles Redd of the bedroom he created for an eleven-year-old. Since floor space in a city apartment is at a premium, Redd brought in a daybed. He covered the walls with Schumacher's cheerful Citrus Garden and the bed in Double Dotty by Peter Fasano. The yellow satin canopy above the bed is by David Haag.

MILES REDD

Two young boys get a versatile space they can grow up in. "I wanted to create a room with beds that could double as sofas as well as offer privacy," says New York-based designer Amy Lau. "So I designed a large amount of hidden storage with complementary areas for display, leaving the central floor space open for the boys to play." The space was finished off with two identical custom desks for the boys to individualize. S. Harris roman shade fabric and Cherner desk chair.

AMY LAU DESIGN

"I wanted to create a room where the client's grandchildren could come and visit and could all stay together," says designer Sara Gilbane. "With a large bedroom there was room for built-in beds but I wanted more than two children to be able stay in here and the windows let in a lot of light so I didn't want to block them with bunk beds. The pullout trundle beds solved this problem." The pale aqua tented walls and ceiling give this room a whimsical airy feeling and help balance the built-ins on one side. John Robshaw textiles on the window treatments and quilts.

SARA GILBANE

"A rug as big as you can go always makes a room feel larger," says Singapore-based designer Elizabeth Hay. "I think people are sometimes tempted to put a small rug in a small room, but this more often than not makes the room feel smaller. We also added bold patterns, textures, and wallpaper, which make it feel bigger and add interest. Since this two-year-old had a separate playroom, this was to be just a cozy bedroom where she would sleep and read." Hay's firm designed the hand blocked pleated lampshade and the wallpaper is from Cole & Son.

ELIZABETH HAY DESIGN

For a girls' shared bedroom, designer Kevin Walsh's client wanted a beautiful classic bedroom heavy on style for her two young daughters, with plenty of storage. Walsh decided on twin beds from Jonathan Adler to keep the room open for extra seating options and room to grow. The wallpaper is from Gracie Studio and linens are from Matouk. The custom-built cabinets are backed in Crosby Stripe in Strawberry from Clarence House.

**KEVIN WALSH,
BEAR HILL INTERIORS**

Julie Hillman used de Gournay's Butterflies pattern in a creamy pink palette on both the walls and the bed's canopy to create a luxurious cocoon and articulate the space. "What I love about this design is that it feels like clouds on the ceiling, which adds to the butterfly forest setting of the room," says Hillman. "I purchased the antique bed from Sotheby's including the original fabric canopy and drapery. I then replicated the style exactly in custom-painted de Gournay fabric. I loved the idea of the walls and the bed matching. The butterfly wallpaper and colors were chosen by the young girl whose room this was going to be. The unique overhead lighting by artist Ayala Serfaty brings a mature sophistication that will endure as the child grows. It was important that I contrast all the pattern with clean, more contemporary elements."

JULIE HILLMAN DESIGN

"It's so important to allow for real life stuff when designing with children in mind," says New York decorator Bella Mancini. "The most important element is that it feels cheerful, casual, and not overdone."

BELLA MANCINI DESIGN

"We never like our children's rooms to be too sweet. We would rather layer them so they can grow with the child as their likes change," says Joe Lucas of Lucas Studio, Inc., who grounded the room with a Krane herringbone wallpaper from Harbinger and a Stark leopard carpet, both in a deep periwinkle color. "None of the furniture is very expensive but we made sure there is color everywhere," adds Lucas, who left the middle of the room open for crucial play area.

LUCAS STUDIO, INC.

This room belongs to a six-year-old girl in New York City and reflects her colorful personality. "I love to make children's rooms happy, whimsical places that help the parents build a fun bedtime story," says its designer, Sara Gilbane, who transformed the vintage birdcage into a chandelier. "Pattern on pattern hides a lot. Nail holes in the walls, spills on the patterned area rug disappear, and all the colors encourage creativity!" The area rug is from Madeline Weinrib.

SARA GILBANE

North Carolina-based designer MA Allen wanted just a hint of coastal for her five-year-old daughter's bedroom at the beach. "I was hunting for a steal on vintage peacock headboards. In the end I found this pair of reproductions on sale at a big box retailer. I went for it and then had them lacquered bright coral." Allen also relied on the smart solution of twin beds: "They are ideal in a room designed for children. As my daughter ages and wants to bring friends to the beach, twin beds are the perfect solution for sleepovers where kids actually sleep!"

MA ALLEN, MA ALLEN INTERIORS

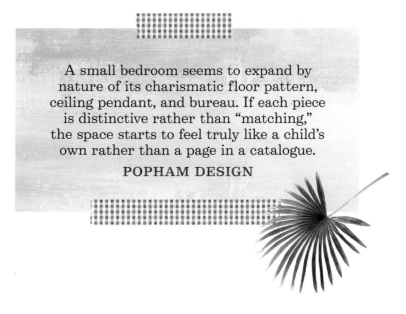

A small bedroom seems to expand by nature of its charismatic floor pattern, ceiling pendant, and bureau. If each piece is distinctive rather than "matching," the space starts to feel truly like a child's own rather than a page in a catalogue.

POPHAM DESIGN

Angie Hranowsky chose a daybed for her eight-year-old daughter's room so she could sleep, play, or read with ease on it. She draped it with a mod pattern from Raol Textiles that gives the old-fashioned idea of a canopy a fun twist. The shag rug once belonged to the child's twin aunts' childhood bedroom.

ANGIE HRANOWSKY

151

Designer Katie Ridder found inspiration for her daughter's bedroom design from a bedroom she visited in Charlottenhof Palace in Potsdam which was tented and carried out completely in blue-and-white stripes. Ridder created her own variation in her family's weekend home by covering the walls and ceiling of the niche in a striped linen trimmed with red grosgrain ribbon. Swedish antiques and accent fabrics in bright primary colors give this room a fresh spin. "Peter and I wanted the bedrooms in our house to be cozy," says Ridder. "We placed our daughter's bed in the niche to make the most of the space."

KATIE RIDDER, DESIGNER
PETER PENNOYER, ARCHITECT

"This room is shared by my two older girls who are twelve and ten," says designer Kate Brodsky of the Hamptons retreat she created for her family of five. "I wanted them to have a room that was not only playful and pretty but also sophisticated enough for guests and the girls as they grow! My friend Jane Scott Hodges of Leontine Linens in New Orleans suggested this charming design from her archives for the blanket covers." The wallpaper and headboard fabric are from Lake August and the gingham curtains are from Schumacher.

KATE RHEINSTEIN BRODSKY

"My priority for this room was to engage the imagination and to inspire—much as I was as a child by the wallpapers with which my father filled our home," says Hannah Cecil Gurney of her three-year-old's London bedroom with its play area. "The hand-painted de Gournay wallpaper depicts the sprawling grasslands of the African savannah, filled with animals rendered in a striking monochrome palette which I love for its non gender-specific theme, so the room can be shared or reinhabited easily." Cecil Gurney offset this palette with very specific accents of bold primary colors, from the vibrant yellow for the custom-built shelving to the deep blue of the curtains trimmed in a rich red. The eighteenth-century bed frame was resized to a child's proportions by Cecil Gurney and upholstered in Dedar's Young and Lovely in Rouge Marinière.

HANNAH CECIL GURNEY

This little girl's bedroom is decorated with a mix of high and low: the furniture comes from Anthropologie while the purple roman shades are custom from Bassett McNab, and the drapes are made from an Hermès fabric. "I have never decorated a child's room in a juvenile way," says its designer, Fawn Galli. "This bedroom is for a girl age three but she could be eight and it would still work." By pairing drapes in Hermès's Equateur Imprimé in Zenith with a sweetly simple headboard, fun becomes timeless.

FAWN GALLI INTERIORS

For a Montecito vacation home, Los Angeles-based designer Melissa Warner Rothblum wanted to create something playful yet functional for two children under ten-years-old. The beachy painted stripes on the walls speak to the beautiful coastal setting. "Big stripes on a wall are bold," says Rothblum. "But because each stripe is identical in size, it feels organized to the eye."

MELISSA WARNER ROTHBLUM

A converted attic space in Arkansas becomes the sleepover bedroom of every child's dreams. Six bunk beds feel like luxurious sleeping cars, complete with their own curtains, shelves, and reading lights. The all white palette on the walls and bed frames heightens the sense of scale and drama, as does the nickel armillary sphere pendant.

KEVIN WALSH, BEAR HILL INTERIORS

Walls and floors are an ideal place to get
playful and reflect your child's distinct
personality. The cozy textures of the rug
and bedding soften the bold expressions
in the large space.

KELLY BEHUN STUDIO

Modern and monochromatic set just
the right tone for an active and growing
boy. Adding a bunk to this small space
optimized its fifteen-foot ceilings
and handy shelving nearby echoes
their design. Lucky Star wallpaper by
Marley+Malek Kids.

**DIANA RICE AND CHELSEA REALE
OF SISSY+MARLEY**

"I wanted a fun space my children could call their own, but not so young a space that when I had adults using the room they couldn't also delight in it," says designer Elizabeth Georgantas, who is the parent of the two girls (ages eleven and twelve) who enjoy it. "This room can work for my children now, then later as teenagers, and hopefully some day possibly for the next generation." She maximized the fun and longevity by incorporating key elements such as accessibility, five hidden closets, and reading nooks at every bed, and with playful intrigue via a bridge and hideaway spots. The hanging reading nook chairs are by Two's Company.

GEORGANTAS DESIGN + DEVELOPMENT

For four kids under the age of twelve, a shared bunk room in their Deer Valley vacation home is the ideal gathering place for both socializing and quiet time. "Although the kids are all sharing a room, we wanted them to have a bit of independence as well," says the designer Melissa Warner Rothblum. "So each of the four bunks (two not pictured) has its own reading light so each child can flip it off and on as needed." Rothblum used the classic Pendleton blanket to bring back memories of summer camp and adventures. "We did our own twist on the look on the custom draperies," adds Rothblum. "The deep navy walls paired with the Pendleton pattern gives a preppy and crisp feeling."

MELISSA WARNER ROTHBLUM

A four-year-old mini fashionista gets a sophisticated space that will grow with her, thanks to the bold graphics of a black and white color scheme. Madeline Weinrib rug and Drop wallpaper backdrop from Marley+Malek Kids.

DIANA RICE AND CHELSEA REALE OF SISSY+MARLEY

A family's penchant for color and whimsy
was continued into their teenage daughter's
bedroom. "After having many lively conversations
about paints and fabrics, we wanted to keep this
bedroom simple, yet with a little drama," says
their designer, Amy Lau. "Through bold bands
of color against a backdrop of white walls
we achieved this. My inspirations were Josef
Hoffmann artwork and color theory." Benjamin
Moore paints added to the fun on the ceiling and
headboard wall and Lau coordinated these areas
with the fabric trim on the roman shades, the
custom Judy Ross pillows, and with the bedding.

AMY LAU DESIGN

"I love using hand blocked wallpaper in a child's bedroom," says designer Fawn Galli. "It gives a space handmade soul." A Restoration Hardware bedside table and an antique rug keep the room feeling grown-up while the overall simplicity isn't intimidating for an eight-year-old.

FAWN GALLI INTERIORS

This tiny room with sloped ceilings belonged
to the youngest of three girls (age seven), so
naturally it was the smallest and least desirable
choice in the house. "I wanted to embrace those
constraints and create a little jewel box hideaway
for her with a custom built-in bed," says designer
Palmer Weiss. "The inside walls are upholstered
and complete with blind cabinet doors to hide all
of her trinkets and treasures." Wall upholstery
and drapery fabric by Rickshaw Designs.

PALMER WEISS

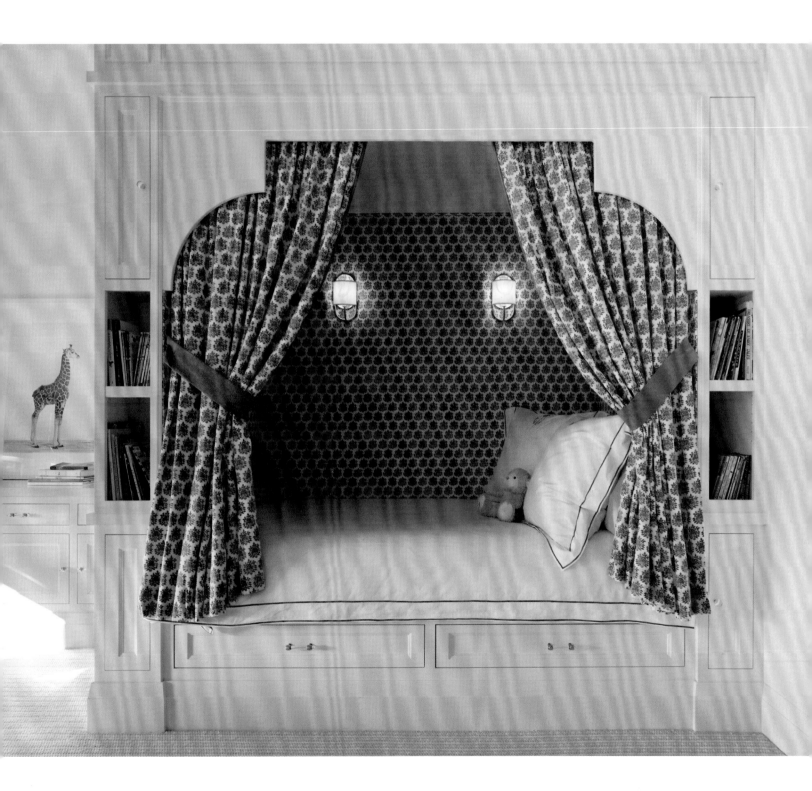

179

"This is our weekend retreat so we left it open instead of chopping it up into smaller closed rooms," says Juli Baker of the nineteenth-century stone farmhouse in Ontario she shares with her husband, John, and their two children, ages six and eight. "We decided to make it a bedroom for the whole family. As well as the children's area, we have a sitting area, fireplace, and a king-size bed. We intentionally keep the large space sparse, so the children have room to use their imaginations to create stuffed animal hotels using old boxes, and blanket forts." Beds from Ikea, bedding from Camomile London, and rocking sheep from Povl Kjer.

JOHN & JULI BAKER, MJÖLK

181

"I wanted to create a timeless and feminine bedroom for my daughter to grow into an independent little girl in," says New York-based designer Natalie Kraiem. "I envisioned a soft blue and white garden. The floral fabrics, soft curves, and porcelain flowers helped create a chic bedroom for many years ahead." Wanting to leave open space for playtime, Kraiem opted to make the Ballard Designs daybed (covered in custom fabric from Ralph Lauren) the focal point, by placing it against the wall and accentuating it with porcelain flowers above. The desk is vintage and Kraiem added knobs from Anthropologie to further personalize it.

NATALIE KRAIEM INTERIORS

where design

play/

study

inspires
imagination

185

design tips

"Wallpaper is a great tool to give design style and personality to a child's space." —fawn galli

"The backdrop or 'envelope' should be more 'mature' than the child's age as children will always add their own age appropriate layers." —jeffrey bilhuber

"In children's bedrooms it's important to have a desk, so homework and paper-writing don't happen in bed (like it does in my daughter's room). I like to have a chest of drawers added into a closet if there isn't room in a bedroom. A bookcase or some storage piece of furniture is important too." —katie ridder

"Play spaces don't have to be relegated to basements and back rooms." —andrew kotchen

"When designing children's spaces, we strive to find a balance between the whimsical and the sophisticated. This way the children do not outgrow their surroundings as they approach their adolescent and teenage years."
—ellie cullman

"Children's rooms should always be playful, and they are a wonderful place to explore with color, but I don't think that they should lack sophistication by any means. On the contrary, a child's room is a unique space where antiques turn into something just a bit more fanciful and can be a great source of inspiration and exploration for a child's mind." —alyssa kapito

"A child's room shouldn't be below any other room in the house in terms of hierarchy of importance. This is where your son or daughter will grow up—it's going to be etched in their memories forever and it's where they will ponder all their important childhood moments and become who they are. You could argue that it's the most critical room to get right and make special." —beata heuman

Scale is a great way to blur the boundaries between reality and kids' imaginations during playtime. Here, a playroom offers the space to play, hide, and dream with cheeky and colorful accents. And there's nothing like a teepee to offer a cozy space within a space for reading. One Kings Lane Kelli knitted poufs, Billings rug in denim by Erin Gates, and teepee by Roller Rabbit.

DESIGN COURTESY OF ONE KINGS LANE

The goal was to create a space that was gender-neutral, playful, and encouraged art. The New York-based design firm Sissy+Marley achieved it via neutral warm tones and by adding interactive pieces like the chalkboard, paper roll, and table and chairs, which encourage the boy and girl who live here to get creative. Ducduc Sebastian chalkboard, George and Willy paper roll, and table and chairs from kinder MODERN.

**DIANA RICE AND CHELSEA REALE
OF SISSY+MARLEY**

A Connecticut family can retreat to their games barn in the country that is as sophisticated as it is playful, thanks to their designer India Mahdavi and a wall size Sol LeWitt line drawing.

INDIA MAHDAVI

"I chose this Lucite desk and chair because visually they don't take up space and have a '70s disco sensibility," says designer Fawn Galli. The Osborne and Little Farfalla wallpaper engages this five-year-old girl with nature, one of Galli's goals.

FAWN GALLI INTERIORS

In her five-year-old daughter's room,
Debbie Propst paired a vintage
rug with Hygge & West's Otomi
wallpaper print for a playful, exotic
vibe that their Boston terrier, Macen,
also enjoys. "I use wallpaper in neutral
tones around the rest of my house
for texture and visual interest,"
says Propst, "and my child's room
is no exception." Dollhouse is from
The Beautiful Bed Company.

**DEBBIE PROPST, ONE KINGS LANE
INTERIOR DESIGN**

"This playhouse is for my beloved grandniece, Elle, who is seven-years-old," says designer Alex Papachristidis. "It was a gift from her grandmother, my sister Ophelia. I wanted to create a small magical world for her, which would be her very own to play in and invite her friends to."

ALEX PAPACHRISTIDIS INTERIORS

198

Elle's
Play House

"All the furniture had to be miniature to match the scale of the house and so I found French antique pieces that worked perfectly." Papachristidis had the floor stenciled in the manner of Baroness Pauline de Rothschild's London bedroom. For the fabrics and wallpaper, he chose Manuel Canovas from Cowtan & Tout, mixing lively prints and toiles in a playful color palette.

ALEX PAPACHRISTIDIS
INTERIORS

"In this space, we wanted to layer color and texture in a way that felt playful and kid friendly for an eight- and an eleven-year-old, while remaining true to the home's fresh, modern aesthetic," says designer Andrew Kotchen of Workshop/APD. Design elements like a knotted Atelier 688 bulb fixture highlight the high ceilings and play off the rope storage baskets, while denim beanbag chairs subtly pick up the color of the sky blue seating. "We gave the kids a lofty, sunny space that feels like a getaway from more "grown-up" areas of the home." Chairs from Design Within Reach.

WORKSHOP/APD

previous pages and opposite: "This playroom for a one-year-old boy and a four-year-old girl was designed to grow with the children as a flexible play space that could also work for school-age children and beyond." *right:* "My goal was to create a fun and safe environment where the children could be creative and make a mess!" says designer Lisa Frantz of Marks & Frantz Interior Design. "So we installed a hardwood floor in the crafts corner of this playroom for easy cleanup. The house's exterior divides this craft area from the main section of the playroom and I really wanted it to feel like its own destination."

LISA FRANTZ FOR MARKS & FRANTZ INTERIOR DESIGN

"We wanted a playroom that blended in with the home's neutral palette," says Diana Rice of the design firm Sissy+Marley. "This space is chic and also accommodating enough that the adults could hang and play a game of chess with their boy and girl, who are both under ten. We optimized toy and art supply storage by creating custom millwork that housed the toys." Ducduc table and chairs, Lucky Star wallpaper by Marley+Malek Kids.

**DIANA RICE AND CHELSEA REALE
OF SISSY+MARLEY**

"This playroom was designed to do triple duty as a craft space, Lego workroom, and movie theater for two children under the age of six," says San Francisco-based designer Palmer Weiss, who wanted a space where kids could make a mess but where everything could easily be put back in place at the end of the day. Art made on the Serena and Lily table then gets pinned up on the Donghia grass cloth walls. "Kids' playrooms do not need a lot of furniture or décor as they really should be more blank canvases for a child's own creativity," says Weiss.

PALMER WEISS

"I love using textiles from around the world to inspire children's curiosity," says Brooklyn-based designer Fawn Galli. Here, for two boys ages three and six, she framed a Mexican textile and dangled a solar system above child-scale furniture to encourage global exploration.

FAWN GALLI INTERIORS

For a family with children ages one through ten, the New York-based design firm Cullman & Kravis set out to create a multipurpose room with a comfortable seating area and a family dining table, both of which are across from an open kitchen. The ceramic jacks installation over the sofa was a whimsical way to add color, dimension, and a bit of humor. The cube end tables were custom-designed by the firm to give stylish storage for toys and conceal clutter. The dark ultrasuede on the sofa is easily cleanable and hides wear and tear. A lightweight and easily movable coffee table functions well for games and its rounded edges are safe for small children.

ALYSSA URBAN, KATIE SUTTON, AND DANI MAZZA OF CULLMAN & KRAVIS ASSOCIATES

Eight sleeping "pods" and two padded "book nooks" create a kind of futuristic sleepaway camp at home for three lucky children that ensures both privacy and socialization, thanks to designer Kelly Behun's ingenious design. Each pod is painted in a bright color that coordinates with the rug. Paint colors used for the pod interiors are in Benjamin Moore's Lazy Sunday, Springhill Green, Waterfall, and Iris Bliss. Rug is from kinder MODERN.

KELLY BEHUN STUDIO

Creating a border of chalkboard paint made this
play kitchen space feel modern and fun. The bold
color combination feels sophisticated and will have
a more enduring presence within an apartment
space, unlike many playrooms painted in childlike
primary colors. Kitchen from BRIO.

**DIANA RICE AND CHELSEA REALE OF
SISSY+MARLEY**

"I wanted to create a whimsical and (most importantly) interactive space for a three-year-old," says stylist and designer Mieke ten Have. "So I really paid attention to scale when designing this room for my client, Maisonette: stuffed animals and toys are commensurate with the size of toddlers. There had to be plenty of places to sit down, a table for drawing, toys to ride on, and books to reach. As in any room, I considered scale and proportion." A neutral wall color makes the bold, colorful toys and games in the room especially impactful.

MIEKE TEN HAVE

Designer Fawn Galli pairs sophisticated fabrics
with children's furniture to create a timeless
feel for this six-year-old girl's work area.
"I chose to make roman shades out of Florence
Broadhurst's fabric Peacock Feather because
the peacocks are exotic, mature, and playful."

FAWN GALLI INTERIORS

Designer Bella Mancini wanted to indulge her seven-year-old daughter's love for color and Mancini's own love for textiles with a daybed that's covered with vintage patterns that embrace a youthful, bohemian spirit. Its trundle makes it ideal for sleepovers.

BELLA MANCINI DESIGN

"My son, Christoph, has known this room exactly as it is from his first birthday to his eleventh," says his father, designer Jeffrey Bilhuber. "I'm as happy with the Albert Hadley wallpaper as he is and it will remain the cornerstone through each of the room's inevitable incarnations."

JEFFREY BILHUBER

Designer Mark Cunningham created an extended window seat to free up the central space in this child's room to allow for more playing; it is also wide enough to accommodate an afternoon dreamer.

DESIGN BY MARK CUNNINGHAM INC.

credits

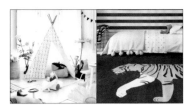
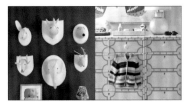

PAGE 39
designer: Ross Cassidy
photographer: Shade Degges

PAGE 40
designer: Kari McIntosh
photographer: Juli Milos

PAGE 43
designer: Palmer Weiss
photographer: Matthew Millman

PAGES 44–45
designer: Griffith Blythe Interiors
photographer: Griffith Blythe Interiors

PAGES 46–47
designer: Jennie Bishop, Studio Gild
photographer: Mike Schwartz

PAGE 48
designer: Lisa Sherry of Lisa Sherry Interieurs
photographer: Makenzie Loli

PAGE 51
designer and photographer: Hannah Soboroff Shargal, EEMA Studio

PAGES 52–53
designer: Dina Bandman
photographer: Christopher Stark

bedrooms

PAGES 58–59
detail of page 60

PAGE 60
designer: Celerie Kemble
photographer: Douglas Friedman

PAGE 63
designers: Suysel dePedro Cunningham and Anne Maxwell Foster of Tilton Fenwick
photographer: Trevor Tondro

PAGE 64
designer: Barrie Benson Interior Design
photographer: Chris Edwards

PAGES 66–67
architect: Tim Barber, Tim Barber, Ltd.
designer: Kristen Panitch
photographer: Jean Randazzo

PAGE 68
designer: Sara Gilbane
photographer: Zach Desart

PAGE 71
designer: David A. Land and Rumaan Alam
photographer: David Land/OTTO

PAGE 105
designer: Elizabeth Hay Design
photographer: Alecia Neo

PAGE 106
designer: Debbie Propst, One Kings Lane Interior Design
photographer: Stacey Bewkes

PAGES 108–109
designer: David Netto
architect: Hottenroth & Joseph
photographer: Pieter Estersohn (Art Department)

PAGES 110–111
designer: Sara McCann and Ashley Warren for McCann Design Group
photographer: © Sargent Photo

PAGE 112
designer: Cameron Ruppert Interiors
photographer: Angie Seckinger

PAGES 114–115
photographer: Stacey Bewkes

PAGE 116
designer: Jett Thompson HOME
photographer: David O. Marlow

PAGES 118–119
designer: Katie Brown and The Katie Brown Workshop with the help of Brice Gillard and Stephanie DiTullio
photographer: David Land/OTTO

PAGE 121
designer: Bella Mancini Design
photographer: Ball & Albanese

PAGE 122
designer: Lisa Sherry of Lisa Sherry Interieurs
photographer: Mekenzie Loli

PAGE 125
designer: Barrie Benson Interior Design
photographer: Brie Williams

PAGES 126–127
designer: Diana Rice and Chelsea Reale of Sissy+Marley
photographer: Marco Ricca

PAGE 128
designer: Miles Redd
photographer: David Haag

PAGE 131
designer: Amy Lau Design
photographer: Mark Roskams

PAGES 132–133
designer: Sara Gilbane
photographer: Carmel Brantley

PAGE 135
designer: Elizabeth Hay Design
photographer: Alecia Neo

PAGES 136–137
designer: Kevin Walsh, Bear Hill Interiors
photographer: Rett Peek

PAGE 139
designer: Julie Hillman Design
photographer: Manolo Yllera

PAGES 140–141
designer: Bella Mancini Design
photographer: Ball & Albanese

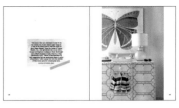

PAGE 143
designer: Lucas Studio, Inc.
photographer: Karyn Millet

PAGE 144
designer: Sara Gilbane
photographer: Zach Desart

PAGES 146–147
designer: MA Allen, MA Allen Interiors
photographer: Eve Hobgood

PAGE 148
designer: Popham Design
photographer: Richard Powers

PAGE 151
designer: Angie Hranowsky
photographer: Julia Lynn

PAGE 152
designer: Katie Ridder
architect: Peter Pennoyer
photographer: Pieter Estersohn (Art
Department)

PAGES 154–155
designer: Kate Rheinstein Brodsky
photographer: Stacey Bewkes

PAGES 156–157
designer: Hannah Cecil Gurney
photographer: Douglas Friedman

PAGE 159
designer: Fawn Galli Interiors
photographer: Costa Picadas

PAGES 160–161
designer: Melissa Warner Rothblum
photographer: Grey Crawford

PAGE 163
designer: Kevin Walsh, Bear Hill
Interiors
photographer: Rett Peek

PAGE 164
designer: Kelly Behun STUDIO
photographer: Richard Powers

PAGE 167
designer: Diana Rice and Chelsea Reale
of Sissy+Marley
photographer: Marco Ricca

PAGES 168 & 169
designer: GEORGANTAS Design + Development
photographer: Stacey Bewkes

PAGES 170–171
designer: Melissa Warner Rothblum
photographer: Kimberly Gavin

PAGE 172
designer: Diana Rice and Chelsea Reale of Sissy+Marley
photographer: Marco Ricca

PAGE 175
designer: Amy Lau Design
photographer: Kim Sargent

PAGE 176
designer: Fawn Galli Interiors
photographer: Costa Picadas

PAGE 179
designer: Palmer Weiss
photographer: Matthew Millman

PAGES 180–181
designer: John & Juli Baker, Mjölk
photographer: Andrew Rowat

PAGES 182–183
designer: Natalie Kraiem Interiors
photographer: Patrick Cline

play/study

PAGES 188–189
design courtesy of One Kings Lane
photographer: Frank Tribble for One Kings Lane

PAGE 190
designer: Diana Rice and Chelsea Reale of Sissy+Marley
photographer: Marco Ricca

PAGES 192–193
designer: India Mahdavi
photographer: Jason Schmidt

PAGE 195
designer: Fawn Galli Interiors
photographer: Costa Picadas

PAGE 196
designer: Debbie Propst, One Kings Lane Interior Design
photographer: Stacey Bewkes

PAGES 198–199
designer: Alex Papachristidis Interiors
photographer: Stacey Bewkes

PAGES 200–201
designer: Alex Papachristidis Interiors
photographer: Stacey Bewkes

PAGE 202
designer: Workshop/APD
photographer: Donna Dotan Photography

PAGES 204–205
designer: Lisa Frantz for Marks & Frantz
Interior Design
photographer: Marco Ricca

PAGES 206–207
designer: Lisa Frantz for Marks & Frantz
Interior Design
photographer: Marco Ricca

PAGE 208
designer: Diana Rice and Chelsea Reale
of Sissy+Marley
photographer: Marco Ricca

PAGES 210–211
designer: Palmer Weiss
photographer: Matthew Millman

PAGE 212
designer: Fawn Galli Interiors
photographer: Costa Picadas

PAGES 214–215
designer: Alyssa Urban, Katie Sutton,
and Dani Mazza of Cullman & Kravis
Associates
photographer: Eric Piasecki/OTTO

PAGES 216–217
designer: Kelly Behun STUDIO
photographer: Stephen Kent Johnson

PAGE 219
designer: Diana Rice and Chelsea Reale
of Sissy+Marley
photographer: Marco Ricca

PAGES 220–221
designer: Mieke ten Have
photographer: Scott Irvine

PAGE 222
designer: Fawn Galli Interiors
photographer: Costa Picadas

PAGES 224–225
designer: Bella Mancini Design
photographer: Ball & Albanese

PAGE 226
designer: Jeffrey Bilhuber
photographer: Stacey Bewkes

PAGES 228–229
designer: Mark Cunningham Inc.
photographer: Richard Powers

thank you

As always I want to thank my amazing editor, Ellen Nidy. Even though our children have grown since our first *Room for Children* book, your insightfulness never waivers. And thank you to my superstar art director, Kayleigh Jankowski, who instinctively brings structure and beauty to whatever is submitted to her.

Thank you, also, to Charles Miers for always believing in my future ideas and not just my past ones.

A book like this is only as vibrant as all the designers and hosts who allow me to share their images, so thank you to everyone!

Finally, thank you to Stacey Bewkes who generously shared so many of her wonderful photographs and who is always by my side as we capture the very best in design.